THE SCIENCE OF NATURAL DISASTERS

THE SCIENCE OF VOLCANIC ERUPTIONS

Alicia Z. Klepeis

Published in 2020 by Cavendish Square Publishing, LLC
243 5th Avenue, Suite 136, New York, NY 10016

First Edition

Library of Congress Cataloging-in-Publication Data

Names: Klepeis, Alicia Z.
Title: The science of volcanic eruptions / Alicia Z. Klepeis.
Description: New York : Cavendish Square Publishing, 2020. | Series: The science of natural disasters | Includes glossary and index.
Identifiers: ISBN 9781502646583 (pbk.) | ISBN 9781502646606 (library bound) | ISBN 9781502646590 (6pack) | ISBN 9781502646613 (ebook)
Subjects: LCSH: Volcanic eruptions--Juvenile literature. | Volcanoes--Juvenile literature.
Classification: LCC QE521.3 K48 2020 | DDC 551.22--dc23

Editorial Director: David McNamara
Editor: Kristen Susienka
Copy Editor: Nathan Heidelberger
Associate Art Director: Alan Sliwinski
Designer: Ginny Kemmerer
Production Coordinator: Karol Szymczuk
Photo Research: J8 Media

The photographs in this book are used by permission and through the courtesy of: : Cover Ammit/Alamy Stock Photo; p. 1 background (and used throughout the book) Kelin/Shutterstock.com; p. 4 Shayes17/E+/Getty Images; p. 5 lightning background (and used throughout the book) Lightkite/Shutterstock.com; p. 7 Kitnha/Shutterstock.com; p. 8 Brian Overcast/Alamy Stock Photo; p. 9 Guitar photographer/Shutterstock.com; p. 10 Chris W Anderson/Shutterstock.com; p. 11 Vectorlight/Shutterstock.com; p. 12 Aldona Griskeviciene/Shutterstock.com; p. 14 TIim Brown/Science Source; p. 15 Chirokung/Shutterstock.com; p. 16 Ellen Bronstayn/Shutterstock.com; p. 17 LukaKikina/Shutterstock.com; p. 19 Lissandra Melo/Shutterstock.com; p. 20 Jim Sugar/Corbis/Getty Images; p. 22 The Yomiuri Shimbun/AP Images; p. 24 USGS/Wikimedia Commons/File:The Heat is On.jpg/Public Domain; p. 26 Koichi Kamoshida/Getty Images.

Printed in the United States of America

CONTENTS

CHAPTER 1 What's a Volcano Like? 5

CHAPTER 2 How Volcanoes Form 13

CHAPTER 3 Getting Ready for Volcanic Eruptions 23

Glossary 29

Find Out More 30

Index 31

About the Author 32

The Fuego volcano in Antigua, Guatemala, erupted in 2016.

CHAPTER 1

WHAT'S A VOLCANO LIKE?

Imagine you're a farmer living in Asia. One morning, while planting your fields, you hear rumbling and roaring sounds. Then BOOM! You look up. In the distance, you see a volcano in the process of erupting. Ash, rock, and gas blast into the air. You also spy something that's reddish-orange. It's **lava** flowing from the volcano. You hope it doesn't come near your fields or your home. As the eruption continues, the sky starts to darken. Smoke and dust from the volcano block the sun. How scary!

Volcano Basics

Volcanoes can change landscapes. They can upset or hurt people, animals, or buildings. But what is a volcano? A volcano is a **vent**, or opening, in Earth's crust. Melted or hot rock and gases come out of a volcano.

Earth's surface is made up of many pieces. These pieces are always moving. This causes volcanoes to form.

DID YOU KNOW?

The word "volcano" comes from Roman times. It's named after the Roman god Vulcan. He was the god of fire. It was believed he had power over volcanoes.

Where Volcanoes Are Found

Volcanoes are located all over the world. There are volcanoes on every continent. However, some places have more volcanoes than others. The United States has more volcanoes than any other country. Russia and Indonesia come in second and third place. Western Canada also has many volcanoes.

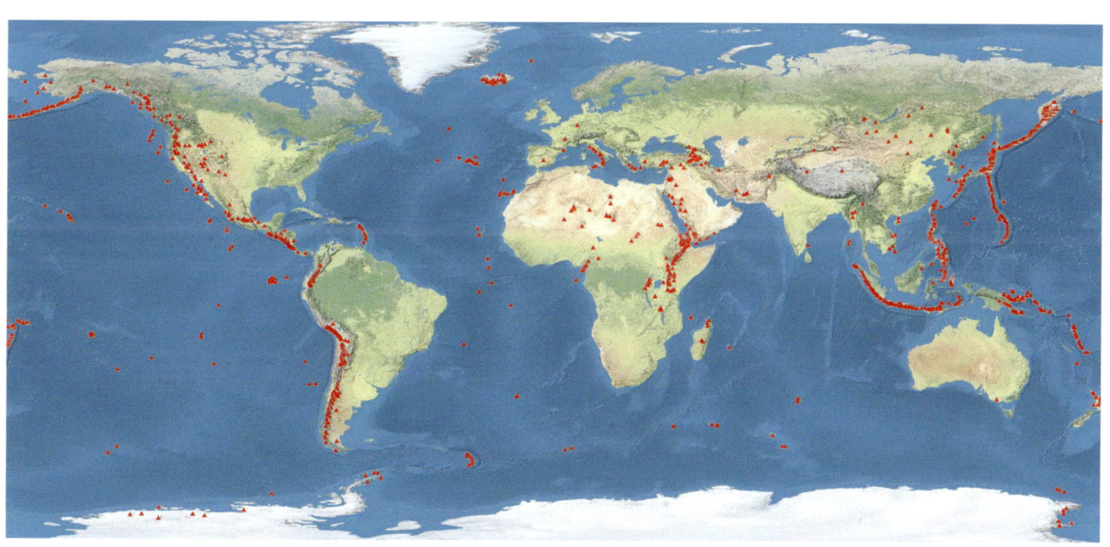

In this map of volcanoes around the world, the red dots show where volcanoes are.

Parícutin is a cinder cone volcano located in Mexico. It emerged suddenly from a farmer's field in 1943.

Types of Volcanoes

There are three main kinds of volcanoes. The simplest kind of volcano is a cinder cone. It is built from blobs and small pieces of lava thrown out from one vent. As the lava blows into the air, it breaks up into tiny pieces.

DID YOU KNOW?

There are approximately 1,500 active volcanoes around the world. Over 170 of these are located in the United States.

These fall around the vent, forming a circular or oval cone. Many volcanoes in western North America are cinder cones.

A stratovolcano has steep sides made up of layers of lava and ash. It's also called a composite volcano. A stratovolcano is like a layer cake. It can be tall—more than 8,000 feet (2,438 meters) high. Mount Fuji in Japan and Mount Shasta in California are composite volcanoes.

Mount Fuji is Japan's tallest mountain. It is also an active composite volcano, or stratovolcano, but it has not erupted since 1707.

Located on the island of Hawaii, Mauna Loa is the biggest active volcano on Earth. It last erupted in 1984. It is also a shield volcano.

A shield volcano has a cone shape with a broad base and sides that slope. These volcanoes are almost completely built from lava. Mauna Kea and Kilauea in Hawaii are examples.

Asleep or Awake?

Around the world, some volcanoes can erupt right now. Those are called active volcanoes. Other volcanoes might not have erupted for a long time, but they could! Those are called dormant volcanoes. Volcanoes that will never erupt again are called extinct volcanoes.

THE RING OF FIRE

There is an important chain of volcanoes that stretches around the Pacific Ocean. It is called the Ring of Fire. It's not a perfect ring shape, but more like a horseshoe. The Ring of Fire is huge. It stretches for 25,000 miles (40,000 kilometers). It runs from New Zealand and Japan, across the Bering Strait, down along the North American coast, and all the way to South America's southern tip. More than 450 volcanoes make up the Ring of Fire. Many are active, but some are dormant.

The Ring of Fire is shown in red on this world map.

This illustration shows magma rising through a volcano's vents during an eruption.

CHAPTER 2

HOW VOLCANOES FORM

When you see a volcano, it looks like it starts on the ground and reaches up to the sky. But actually, volcanoes start below Earth's surface. The outer layer of Earth is called the crust. The crust is broken into huge pieces known as **tectonic plates**. These pieces fit together like a puzzle. Most volcanoes are found where two (or more) plates meet.

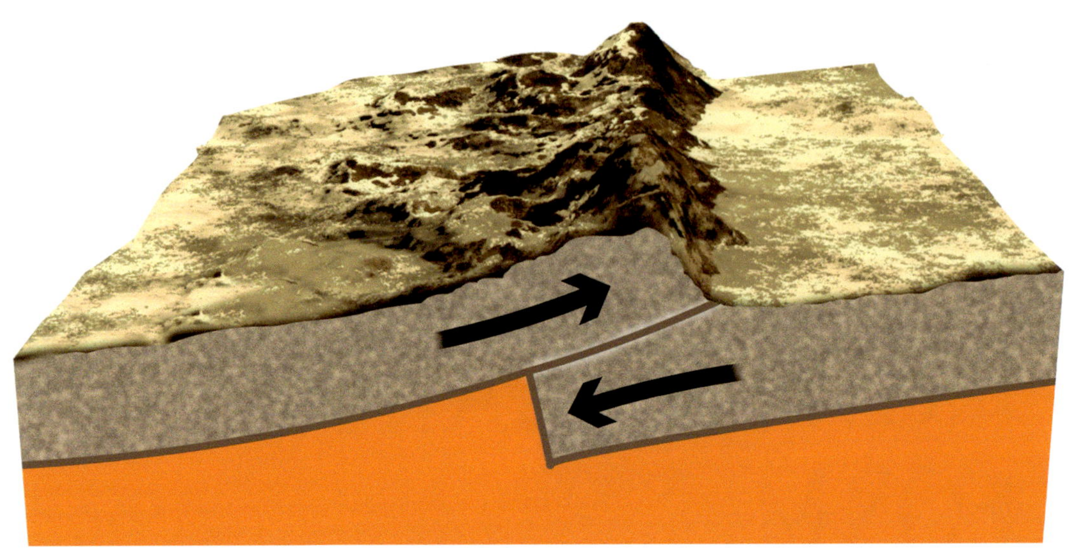

Here, one tectonic plate moves under another as they collide. This process can form volcanoes and cause earthquakes.

Crashing Plates Make Volcanoes

Sometimes tectonic plates crash into each other. When that happens, the heavier plate slips underneath the lighter one. This creates volcanoes and earthquakes. Mount Ruapehu in New Zealand was formed when the Pacific Plate and the Australian Plate crashed into each other. Other volcanoes were created this way too.

What Lies Below

Beneath Earth's crust is a thick layer of rock called the mantle. It's so hot there that rock melts like a candy bar on a toasty day. This thick liquid rock is called **magma**. Magma rises up through the crust toward Earth's surface.

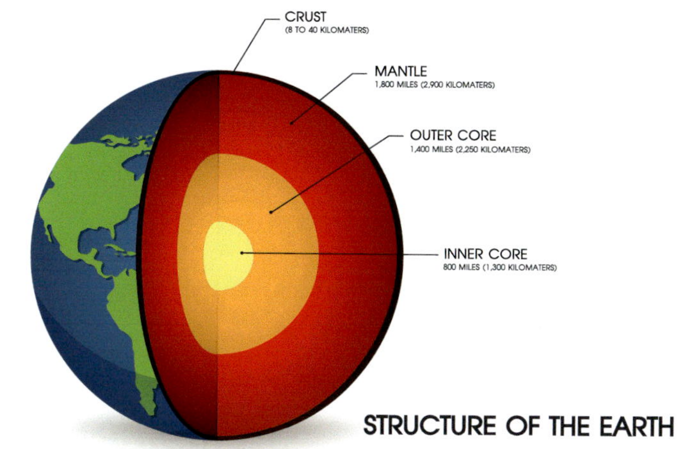

This diagram shows the four layers of planet Earth. Volcanoes are openings in the outer layer, or crust.

As magma moves upward, it collects in a pool called a **magma chamber**. This is an underground storage area for magma. The magma stays there until something happens to make a volcano erupt.

Why and How Volcanoes Erupt

Magma fills up the chamber and creates pressure. Sometimes the pressure gets so high that it makes the volcano burst. This is called a volcanic eruption.

Think of a volcanic eruption like when you drink a soft drink. The more you drink, the more gas builds up inside your body. Soon, the gas makes you burp. The burp releases pressure inside you. In that same way, a volcanic eruption reduces pressure inside a magma chamber. However, sometimes so much magma is

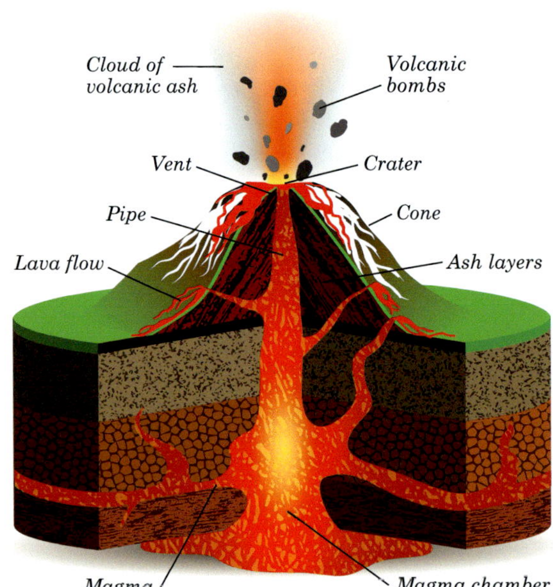

A volcano has many parts, as illustrated here.

thrown out that the magma chamber collapses. A **caldera** can form. **Crater** Lake in Oregon is a famous caldera.

Russia's Karymsky volcano is erupting violently in this photo. Its last known eruption was in 2018.

During an eruption, a volcano throws out gases, ash, and rock. Most magma escapes through a main opening, called a vent. But magma can also escape through smaller vents. When magma leaves a volcano, it is called lava.

DID YOU KNOW?

There are volcanoes on planets besides Earth. The largest volcano in our solar system is Olympus Mons on Mars. It's about the size of the US state of Arizona!

Volcanoes Erupt in Different Ways

All volcanoes have a magma chamber and vents. However, they don't all erupt the same way. Some volcanoes erupt violently. They can create avalanches of ash, hot volcanic **debris**, and gas. They can destroy anything in their path. Mount Saint Helens in Washington State erupted violently in 1980.

Some volcanoes don't erupt violently. Instead, lava only pours out of the volcano. Because the lava is not traveling fast, this type of eruption destroys fewer things. Mauna Loa in Hawaii erupts this way.

Hot springs, geysers, and mud pools all show the thermal activity of the volcano located at Yellowstone National Park.

Hot Spots and Supervolcanoes

Not all volcanoes are found where tectonic plates meet. Some are in the middle of a plate where the magma below is very hot. This is called a hot spot. When a tectonic plate moves over a hot spot, the magma can

DID YOU KNOW?

Located in Hawaii, Kilauea has continuously erupted on Earth the longest. Lava has been spilling from its Puu Oo crater since 1983!

Molten lava spews out from Puu Oo, a volcanic vent of Kilauea volcano.

melt through it. The magma pushes through cracks in Earth's crust here. This forms volcanoes. Hot spots have made volcanoes in Hawaii and other places. They have also made supervolcanoes. A supervolcano is a huge volcano. It is so large that it could wipe out humankind if it erupts.

DID YOU KNOW?

One of the largest supervolcanoes today is in the United States. It is found in Yellowstone National Park. If it erupts, it could destroy or damage all of North America—and even the entire world.

VOLCANIC EXPLOSIVITY INDEX

The Volcanic Explosivity Index (or VEI) helps scientists measure a volcanic eruption. It has scores of 0 to 8. The lower the score number, the less dangerous a volcanic eruption is.

Score	Description	Frequency
0–1	quiet but producing lava	occurs frequently
2–4	small to moderate explosion	occurs every year somewhere in world
5	explosive blast	occurs every decade or so
6	explosive blast	once in 100 years
7	explosive blast	once in 1,000 years
8	explosive blast	once in 10,000 years or less

Each number on the scale is ten times stronger than the one above it. So a VEI 5 eruption is ten times stronger than a VEI 4 eruption.

During this 2015 evacuation drill in Japan, participants walk down Mount Fuji wearing protective masks and hard hats.

CHAPTER 3

GETTING READY FOR VOLCANIC ERUPTIONS

When a volcano is ready to erupt, there's nothing people can do to stop it. However, that doesn't mean people can't predict or prepare for volcanic eruptions.

Learning from the Past

Volcanologists are scientists who study volcanoes. They look at what happened in past eruptions. This can help them guess how a volcano might act in the future. At the Hawaiian Volcano Observatory, researchers have studied the behavior of Kilauea since the early 1900s. Today, they can predict this volcano's eruptions very well.

Warning Signs

There are warning signs before volcanoes erupt. You can see some signs. For example, lots of gas and ash may come out of a volcano's crater. Small earthquakes are another sign. An instrument called a seismograph

A scientist collects a lava sample from an active volcano in Hawaii.

DID YOU KNOW?

In 2010, Indonesia's Mount Merapi erupted. It was the volcano's worst eruption in one hundred years. Thanks to technology that predicted the eruption, over seventy thousand people got to safety in time.

measures and records earthquakes. It measures how strong they are and how long they last. Lots of earthquakes around a volcano could mean it will erupt soon.

Other technologies measure a volcano's pressure. Radar satellite systems and GPS can sense when the pressure inside magma chambers increases. If the pressure gets high enough, a volcanic eruption will happen.

Elementary school children wear flame-proof hoods during a disaster drill in Japan.

Preparing for Volcanic Eruptions

Around the world, millions of people live close to active volcanoes. It is important for them to know what to do if an eruption happens.

Many cities near volcanoes have an emergency plan. This plan tells people to leave the city. It gives them places to go away from the city. It tells them how to get there safely. Other cities have preparation drills. This means people practice what to do if a volcanic eruption is happening in their city. In Japan, children in school put on hard hats or special clothing to protect themselves. Adults put up huge concrete blocks to keep lava away.

Building Strong

In cities where volcanic eruptions can happen, people build houses and workplaces differently. They might have houses with slanted roofs. A slanted roof lets volcanic ash slide off the building. This can help keep a roof from collapsing after an eruption.

Engineers are creating new building materials that can better survive a volcanic eruption. One idea is to build houses on tall sticks. These sticks are called stilts. The stilts would be made from materials that wouldn't melt if lava rushed over them. Thanks to the stilts, the lava could pass underneath the house without damaging it.

DID YOU KNOW?

The last super eruption at Yellowstone happened about 631,000 years ago. Almost half of the United States was covered in a powder of crushed rock and ash.

ROBOTIC TECHNOLOGY AND VOLCANOES

Some volcanoes are underwater instead of on land. Today, robots help human volcanologists study underwater volcanoes. They can go into dangerous places where people cannot. Robots called Wave Gliders gather information about underwater volcanoes. These robots can move in very hot water close to the volcano. They measure different parts of a volcano.

Diving robots like Wave Gliders also study how underwater volcanoes are different from those above ground. For example, rocks thrown out in an eruption sometimes travel farther underwater than on land. The information these robots collect helps scientists better understand how volcanoes erupt.

GLOSSARY

caldera A large hole formed by the collapse of a magma chamber during a volcanic eruption.

crater A hole from which lava escapes in a volcanic eruption.

debris Rocks or other materials that are thrown out of a volcano.

lava Melted rock that comes out of a volcano.

magma Molten rock material under Earth's crust.

magma chamber An underground storage area for magma. It lies below a volcano.

tectonic plates The huge pieces of Earth's crust that move over Earth's mantle.

vent The opening of a volcano where lava and other materials are thrown out.

FIND OUT MORE

Books

Howell, Izzi. *Volcano Geo Facts*. New York: Crabtree Publishing Company, 2018.

Nargi, Lela. *Absolute Expert: Volcanoes*. Washington, DC: National Geographic Partners, LLC, 2018.

Website

Volcanoes

https://www.dkfindout.com/us/earth/volcanoes

This website discusses the different types of volcanoes, explains hot spots, and lets visitors hear a volcano erupt.

Video

Explore Volcanoes with Nat Geo Kids!

https://www.youtube.com/watch?v=Xtkys3-T-Y8

Learn what volcanoes are, how tectonic plates move, and how volcanic eruptions are not all the same.

INDEX

Page numbers in **boldface** refer to images. Entries in **boldface** are glossary terms.

active, 10–11, 26

caldera, 17

cinder cone, 8–9, **8**

crater, **16**, 17, 19, 24

crust, 6, 13, 15, **15**, 20

debris, 18

dormant, 10–11

earthquakes, 14, 24–25

extinct, 10

hot spot, 19–20

lava, **4**, 5, 8–10, **12**, **16**, 17–19, **20**, 21, **24**, 26–27

magma, **12**, 15–17, **16**, 19–20

magma chamber, **12**, 15–18, **16**, 25

mantle, 15, **15**

Mars, 18

prediction, 23–25

preparing, **22**, 26–27, **26**

rating scale, 21

shield volcano, 10, **10**

stratovolcano, 9, **9**

technology, 24–25, 28

tectonic plates, 6, 13–14, **14**, 19–20

underwater, 28

vent, 6, 8–9, **12**, **16**, 17–18

ABOUT THE AUTHOR

Alicia Z. Klepeis began her career at the National Geographic Society. She also taught middle school World Geography for many years before becoming a writer. Klepeis is the author of more than ninety children's books, including *The World's Strangest Foods, Everyday STEM: How Smartphones Work*, and *A Time for Change*. She lives with her family in upstate New York. She visited two volcanoes in Washington State—Mount Saint Helens and Mount Rainier. She also saw the Mount Merapi volcano erupting while visiting the Indonesian island of Java.